PRECIOUS

Award Winning Poetry
Edited by Ted Stanley

HAMMOND HOUSE

PRECIOUS
Award Winning Poetry

Published by
Hammond House Publishing Ltd.
University Centre Grimsby, DN34 5BQ, United Kingdom.

1st Edition: February 2018

ISBN: 978-0-9955702-8-3

All rights reserved. No part of this publication may be reproduced, stored in a retrieval system, or transmitted in any form or by any means, electronic, mechanical, photocopying, recording or otherwise, without the permission of the authors.

The right of the individual writers to be identified as the author of the work to which they have been attributed in this publication has been asserted in accordance with sections 77 and 78 of the Copyright Designs and Patents act 1988.

Compiled and Edited by Ted Stanley
Proofreading and Formatting: Alex Thompson
Cover Design: Ted Stanley

Cover Image *PRECIOU*S, by Deborah Geddes, first exhibited in 2018. Produced by permission of the artist. All rights reserved.
The opinions expressed in this book are entirely those of the individual authors and are not endorsed or supported by the publishers or their sponsors, University Centre Grimsby and Kenwick Park Estates.

Contains language that may be considered unsuitable for a younger audience.

www.hammondhousepublishing.com

PRECIOUS
Award Winning Poetry

Enjoy this eclectic collection of poetry that brings together *award-winning* writers from around the world, each with their own unique interpretation of the theme. PRECIOUS is the second in a series of poetry anthologies, each featuring a different theme and including the top entries from our Annual Poetry Prize.

University Centre Grimsby

Includes the winner of the 2018
International Literary Prize

The opinions expressed in this book are entirely those of the individual authors and are not endorsed or supported by the University Centre Grimsby.

'An imaginative and thoughtful collection of world poetry reflecting a variety of cultures, styles and taste but always resonating with the universal truths that affect us all.' *Steve Jackson*

CONTENTS

ACKNOWLEDGMENTS VI

INTRODUCTION VII

WORDS | ANN ALGIE 1

THE DELICATE FALL | SOLOMON AU YEUNG 3

SNAPSHOTS BY HEART | SOLOMON AU YEUNG 6

SEMPITERNAL SUNSETS | GARRETT BISHOP 8

VASE | DELLA BRETT 9

THE WORLD AND ITS CROWNING OF BEES | JANE BURN 11

CONCERNING WHALES | KEVIN CONNELLY 13

YOU ASK ME | JOANNE DONE 14

THE LAST SONG OF THE MISTLETHRUSH | RUTH FLANAGAN 16

SOLDIER | CHELSEA GANT 19

INDIGO | STACEY GEORGE 20

THE BLACK BOX | SANNA-NOOR KHAN 22

THE YELLOW HAMMER'S NEST | MARK LAWRENCE 24

BLOOD DIAMOND | MEREDITH MARS 26

CONSUMER VALUE | BRUCE MARSLAND 28

THE LANDING | CAROLINA MASSIE 30

YPRES | IAN MCDONALD 33

ENDANGERED WORDS | ALISON MCNULTY 34

Thunder Over Blair Atholl | Laurence Morris 35

2 Poems | Pukhraj Neogi 37

Father | Val Ormrod 39

Did Socrates Dream of Kenny Dalgish? | Ian Rollitt 40

Afternoon Tea | Christine Rowley 42

Lullaby of Old Northumberland | Raymond Salisbury 45

The Elemental Selfhood | Margarita Serafimova 48

Just Another Kid | Samuel Shapiro 49

Sea Trove | Lizzie Smith 50

The Colour Blue | Ted Stanley 51

Pharaoh | Tim Taylor 52

Tiny Choirboy | Laura Theis 53

Jewels | Julia Wallis 54

Dancing in the Rain | Rachel Wilkins 56

Precious Long Ago | Sadie Wood 57

Hourglass | Safiyyah Yacoobali 59

From 'Red Hawthorn-Hedged' | Paul Sutherland 61

ACKNOWLEDGEMENTS

Deborah Geddes, Alex Thompson, Heather Buckby, Ruth Liddemore, Alan, Nicky and the team at Central Services, Leanne Doyle, Jonathon and Katherine Williams-Stanley, Richard Hall, and Michael Edwards. Simon, Lucy, Carol, Heather and Ella in the University Learning Resource Centre for their continued patience advice and support. The University Centre Grimsby and Kenwick Park Estates for sponsoring the 2018 International Literary Prize. Competition Judges, Paul Sutherland and Steve Jackson. Finally, all the writers who submitted such an amazing collection of poetry for this anthology. We are sorry we were unable to include more.

INTRODUCTION

A STRENUOUS ASPECT EXISTS IN ADJUDICATING, but there prevails the pleasure of poetry. As soon as I start to read I sense other peoples and other writers struggle to try to find language to reflect and dramatise their thoughts, feelings and experiences. I may not agree with their structure, images or diction but the adjudicator must accept the sincere intentions and efforts of those he or she rejects. Also, once the mass of reading begins in earnest my conscience is stirred to do justice to these renditions, productions of what Precious, this competition's theme, means.

But selection is often not about analysing the quality of someone's writing. It's about the moment that the reader experiences in a poem: a kind of panic, a vision of Pan as John Burnside describes it, a direct unfiltered experience that shocks the adjudicator. He or she misses a beat or, as one old lady poet portrayed, 'when I read something great, my feet tingle.' My feet tingled a few times reading these entries.

It has to be admitted that choice or selection is highly subjective. Another reader would have experienced a gentle panic from a very different poetic source.

In my case I go back to the poem that stunned and re-read it, trying to deconstruct its elements, untangle the strands of rhythm and style that created surprise, delight and slight shock. Perhaps the jolt is triggered by meeting language, a way of speaking, way of telling, dissimilar from my own, our own, that the joy and excitement can't be dulled or reasoned.

The poem, if often re-visited within limits of adjudicating, never yields its secret power. That stays hidden in the use of vocabulary, imagery and incident concealed in the fabric of the words like a dagger in a cloak. Perhaps it makes an adjudicator blush. At last I submit and bow to its subtle influence and call the poem a winner.

Thank you who entered for your time and precious words, giving me the pleasure of reading. If you failed to be selected, do not be disheartened. Another year and another judge will make different choice.

Paul Sutherland

'Time is precious, but truth is more precious than time.'

Benjamin Disrael

Words

Ann Algie
France

Editor's Choice of International Entries

Words, precious mitochondria of communication,
Silent formless thought, transmuted into sound.
Symbols emerging from the infinite ether of idea-filled minds,
Deliberated, translated and licked into meaning.
Sprinkled onto golden sands, breathed on heather hills,
Slipped over mossy stones and dropped into trickling streams.
Sweetened, round, smooth, pink and perfectly formed, sugar-coated with love,
Delicately placed on dew-softened roses and laugh-crumpled faces,
Lives enriched by words.

Words trapped within, spinning relentlessly in heads,
Weapons of torture and pain, salted, pickled, chewed and minced,
Carelessly uttered, spat out, sprayed amongst cigarette ends,
Lost in graffiti, stuttered with tears, screamed out with pain,
Confused and mixed with saliva, dribbling onto shirt-fronts.
Wielded, wounding, malicious and twisting, gossiping and destroying,
Lives ruined by words.

Words of wisdom, considered, agonised over, jewels in time, searched for and carefully placed,
Passed down through ages, chanted and sung,
Words infused with incense, perfumed, sage-burned and calming.
Whispered over ancient stone floors, in silent halls and drummed across the embers of fires.
Praising, worshiping, delivered as great speeches, hung to and clung to,
Celebrated and cheered, dancing and spinning, words woven into poems,
Lives changed by words.

The Delicate Fall

Solomon Au Yeung
Hong Kong

Editor's Choice of International Entries

holding by bare hands
once a passer-by, the one so easily neglected
those shone the brightest
those 5 petals of white, the white
only found in the snow

the artisan in nature
carved
the five in good proportion
and spread some delicate yellow,
golden, like that on the sweet corns
right at the centre

gently, bearing the silence
extending the changes,
that life in a fragile shell
leaving her long attached branch
of fainted brown.

4 | PRECIOUS

holding the last breath
still, insists on
the consistency of
a liberated artwork
right at the moment when
she finally landed on my hands

Starting to crack
the pieces of
memories
grasping at their best
each last company
the many days together
have now
passed, engulfed in
the forthcoming ashes, gone

wandering
the last float of aroma
blooming
the skin once kissed
in whisper
returning to the motherland
safeguarding this nature's
birth
hoping sometime, soon

another possible meet-up with the
past kin, sharing again the
same roots
to bond this every
short but strong encounter,
& to examine all
the fine but crucial changes...

detached, the falling white
dropped from my palms,
vanished, perhaps
getting used to a new white

Snapshots By Heart

Solomon Au Yeung
Hong Kong

Editor's Choice of International Entries

~we see by our eyes, but much clearer with our hearts~

Shutter blinked, Snap!
that moment when the falling leaves kissed the pond
sketching waves of ripples
using a rare silence
to warn this repetitive rush
of the crowded crowds   to let go
the packed shoulders rubbing in such inharmonious squad   to let go
the dark saturated lumps of metropolitan madness

Shutter blinked, Snap!
that blurry spot
right in front of the Triple Lanterns
a shadow overlapped by two
another bundle of strangers' kisses
leaving behind the burden of stigmatized professionalism deeply
embedded
in a camera

appearing nice & clear

an old couple's promise on an ancient bridge

bearing this precious moment

so they can live out the eternal presence

To grasp by heart

that once blurred vision under the shutter

glancing right at

the crystal clear surface underneath

the bridge

That distant

him, holding up a long-lost smile

slowly taking in

this lightness in relief

To grasp by heart

yet another blurred vision under the shutter

behind the three lanterns

shadows reappearing, flashing

became the typically Chinese revolving lamps, noted

that without the burden bounded by a so-called camera set

catching the shadows only written vaguely in waters

realizing those seemingly familiar blocks

are…wait a second,

once our very close

family, teachers & acquaintances?!

Sempiternal Sunsets

Garrett Bishop
United States

Editor's Choice of International Entries

I remember the warmth of your hand in mine,
    and the grass, pressed against our backs.

I remember the smell of freshly cut grass,
    and that of our little lakeside retreat.

I remember the burning, brilliant gold of the sun,
    and how it burned our eyes and set fire to our skin.

I remember when you'd be the little voice in my ear,
    and you always told me to stay when it was time to leave.

I remember the indescribable feeling of being totally whole,
    and of being content with life in a single instant.

I remember my heart and my mind settling in,
    and staying there forever

I remember laying with you and watching the sky,
    and those sempiternal sunsets.

Vase

Della Brett
United Kingdom

Shortlisted for the 2018 International Literary Prize

An African summer's day which fades to black,

with scratches left like stars upon its sides.

The morning sun illuminates the cracks

of gasping ground in deserts stretching wide.

An empty space concealed by bevelled walls,

sporadic floods to feed fresh cut green shoots,

stretching out to sun light standing tall,

then wilting in a stench of rotting fruit.

Heavy walls which chip and crack with ease,

carry constantly the focus of the room.

Apologise, celebrate or please,

a multitude of colours, bud to bloom.

10 | PRECIOUS

But in the end the focus fades and dies,

and still the sun bleached heirloom will remain.

Hidden in the darkness far from eyes,

until its use is wanted once again.

The World and its Crowning of Bees

Jane Burn
United Kingdom

Shortlisted for the 2018 International Literary Prize

They touch their spindled feet to the trees, dabble

from bloom to bloom, trap the anther's gold

between their toes – rake the priceless dust

against their press, deliver the brilliant atoms

to the new year's growth. Jewels of apple begin

to weight the branches, bulbs of pear and cherry

spark with life. They spill across the crops,

a skittered clutch of amber gems, a busy, buzzing

army, humming their song of honey dreams,

thrumming the neon oil-seed ripe, spindrift of sparks

shimmering the fields. The cosset of elderflower

waits to shape into sprays of delicious beads –

the blossom's ovary waits for the bringing of seed,

waits to birth her gem of berry, offering up its sweet.

12 | PRECIOUS

The world would hush without this waggle dance –

each chain of existence linked by their waltzing speech.
The cabouchons of almond, raised to nourish your cakes,
the humble humps of turnip, hushed like pearls beneath

the earth's tongue – the cows on clover thank the bees
for their ivory wells of scented milk. If they stay to rest
on your shoulder, wear them as you would a topaz brooch –

from out of the planet's cache has come this valuable thing.
Offer them spoons of candied drink for they have spent
their hours in labour, powdering germ on the land.

Concerning Whales

Kevin Connelly
Ireland

Shortlisted for the 2018 International Literary Prize

These are some signs of the Great Whales presence:

still water, suddenly calm, everything

hushed, quiet, ripples elsewhere but here it is tense.

Then know that soon she will rise and so bring

to the surface before your very eyes

a lesson on life, scale, perspective.

Our own self-centred view is hardly wise,

respect for others always good to give.

Concerning whales these are some things I know -

among the wondrous things I have learned,

look for the fountain sprayed from below

for that miracle, I have ofttimes sailed.

Then follow the birds, let them be your guide,

gannets are fishing where the whales also dive.

You Ask Me

Joanna Done
United Kingdom

Shortlisted for the 2018 International Literary Prize

Do I look alright?

Twisting round,
Smoothing down.

Darling child –
Don't ask me that question.
I can't answer

When I look at you,
I see the tiny head
Cupped in my hand.

Feel each toe,
Squeezed between,
Finger and thumb.

Hear the world,
Smash into fragments,
At your wail.

Know the thud

Of my heart,

As I count you in your beds.

From your hair,

I see sparklers,

The night sky lit –

By a thousand screaming stars

From your palms,

There is water rushing

Sharply gushing

Knife bright.

I know infinite love,

Neither growing nor dying

Darling girl,

Dearest boy,

The slant of your cheek

And that half-smile –

Are miracles of now and before,

Cresting like a mountain –

Wide and blue

As any ocean

Do not ask me

Please

If you look alright

When you have my universe dancing in your eyes.

The Last Song of the Mistlethrush

Ruth Flanagan
United Kingdom

Shortlisted for the 2018 International Literary Prize

Upon this spot, in days of old, a Mistle Thrush, so I've been told,
Would perch high in a tall, oak tree and sing of life's rich tapestry.

He sang of bees and butterflies, of morning dew and azure skies.
Of maidens dancing at the fayre with daisy garlands in their hair.
Of joyful faces as they danced, of rosy cheeks and sweet romance,
And long, green grass where lovers lay and kissed as summer slipped away.

Soon the Harvest Moon would glow and paint the corn in gold below.
And as the crop was gathered in, he'd look across the fields and sing.

He sang of carpets on the ground, of crisp, bright leaves in red and brown.
Of fattened pigs with rounded bellies and wild fruits and bramble jelly.
Of happy boys who came and played and chased each other through the glade.

Who laughed while dark'ning evenings crept and spring and summer softly slept.

Next the winter winds would blow and from the north there came the snow.
And still he'd watch the whole day long and fill the heavens with his song.

He sang of footprints in the snow, of people walking to and fro.
The smell of roast goose o'er the fire, the sound of bells and Christmas choirs.
And when the chill began to bite, he'd sing of trees with candle lights.
Of presents waiting on the floor and wreaths of holly on the door.

Spring would come around again, then summer sun, then autumn rain.
And there he'd be, up in the tree, singing his song to you and me.

But one dark day, we went with blades and felled the trees that lined the glade.
From all about there came the sound of great trees tumbling to the ground.
Then as his nest was sawn apart, a shard of steel tore through his heart.
He dropped his head and flapped his wings and as he died, this song did sing.

He sang of Mother Nature's tears, of all her hopes, now turned to fears.

18 | PRECIOUS

Of barren lands and dried up seas, of stumps that stand instead of trees.
Where song no longer fills the air and silence stretches everywhere.
He rolled his eyes towards the sky and begged us stop and asked us why.
"Were they not good, those days," he cried, "when all our needs, the Earth supplied?
Then maidens danced and lovers kissed and autumn leaves were bright and crisp,
And Mistle Thrushes sang in trees and all these precious things were free.
You should have cherished what was thine and shared Earth's gifts and left me mine."

Soldier

Chelsea Gant
United Kingdom

Shortlisted for the 2018 International Literary Prize

Stuck on a verse, stuck on a line,
Stuck on half a boy, with half a line and half a gram to make magic in half a mortal minute.
Oh, the harshness of the halves that halve you in half.
The secret runs in circuits of conspiracy and combat and capital gain
Stuck in a coma flinching from le coup de main.
Breath in, breath out, you will be repaired,
Whisper to the conditioned and brown universe that you are scarred but not scared,
And hear me
"Wake up front line boy,
You're alive, I'm by your side."

Indigo

Stacey George
United Kingdom

3rd Place in the 2018 International Poetry Prize

The scan reveals you like a pearl:
Precious, three years in the making.
Still months before we meet sweet girl,

But you'll be worth all the waiting.
Revered, you're loved so much and prized;
Precious, three years in the making.

I dream of gazing in your eyes
Of deepest blue: like ancient dye,
Revered. You're loved so much and prized

Already. I wonder am I
Strong enough to give you the name
Of deepest blue - like ancient dye

Slow-made. It's my turn to proclaim;
As I catch my breath and stay so

Strong - enough to give you the name

I'd known for years. Dear Indigo,
The scan reveals you like a pearl,
As I catch my breath and stay so
Still, months before we meet sweet girl.

The Black Box

Sanna-Noor Khan
United Kingdom

Shortlisted for the 2018 International Literary Prize

It occupies a space in my head,

It is filled with 30 years of negative experiences.

There's no need to process them I had thought,

Just put them in the box each time.

Years of supply have caused it to mutate,

Now a monster with an increasing appetite.

With time it has also become faulty,

Often it opens up without my consent,

Usually in response to a hurtful word or trigger.

The contents try and escape all at once,

From its big gaping mouth.

If I'm lucky I can snap it shut quickly,

Other times I toss and turn all night,

Chasing the bad dreams one by one.

Now the time has come.

I've got to stop it from growing,

I may even have to cease it from existing.

Maybe I could smash it to pieces,

Then slowly recycle all the emotions,

But I don't want to relive those memories,

The shame, the guilt, the tears.

I have no choice really,

For one day it will consume me.

It won't be inside me.

It will be me.

The black box.

The Yellow Hammer's Nest

Mark Lawrence
United Kingdom

Shortlisted for the 2018 International Literary Prize

You cannot see this treasure,

Bramble's impenetrable fortress estate,

Safeguarding its secret,

With Defences to create

Refuge for a million,

In the recesses of thorns,

Living reasons teach pin point perfection,

This season's army will be born.

Within its natural selection

From the chosen tools of grass,

Spider's net cemented,

A work of art, world class

This brief cavity lease rented,

Nature's nest lesson

Well Represented.

Tucked away, untidy,

With doorstep that lies,

Leaving for the wise

Prized nettle protection,

Stinging sweet surprise.

Four marbled eggs past folklore tells,

Vivid immense patterns,

Vincent Van Gogh will dwell

To swell those eyes and drop open jaws,

The Scribbling lark, the artist,

Painting rich free to explore,

In its castle of thorns spewing colours

On fragile Shells you can't ignore.

Blood Diamond

Meredith Mars
United Kingdom

Shortlisted for the 2018 International Literary Prize

There's treasure buried in this chest-
Caged beneath my ribs,
There's no X to mark the spot-
Just a scar shaped like a kiss.

Under a shield of bone-
Sits a jewel crystal clear;
My dazzling diamond heart,
Forged in pressure, heat, and tears.

Kaleidoscopic spinning top-
Glitters, gleams, and glows.
Refracted light distracts the eye-
From studying too close.

There's nothing lacking in her lustre,
Not a blemish to be found.

Timeless and tenacious,
She's the toughest heart around.

At least, that's what I tell myself-
As I lie alone in bed,
Wondering if I'd be better with-
A rhinestone heart instead.

At least with rhinestones on my sleeve-
I might draw less attention,
Be less exposed and vulnerable-
To those with ill intentions.

But diamonds are forever,
Hearts of gold are soft,
So I'll keep my ornate organ-
And I'll gladly pay the cost.

Consumer Value

Bruce Marsland
United States

Shortlisted for the 2018 International Literary Prize

'The raw materials for phones and computers are mined by underpaid and overworked Congolese teenagers, and those materials are assembled by underpaid and overworked Chinese teenagers.'
– The Huffington Post, 10 November 2014

How many lives is my smartphone worth?
    Calculator has no app for that,
    for counting missing digits, limbs,
    under-age starvation waged by conflict
    minerals, sourced for the bottom line,
    boxed like my phone, undocumented
    in assembly line illiteracy, no suicide note.

'More than a year after 29 people were trapped in a fire at a garment factory in Bangladesh used by well-known American clothing brands, an ABC News investigation found the retailers right back in business at the factory.'
– ABC News, 21 March 2012

How many deaths is my sweatshirt worth?
>   Designers have no logo for that,
>   for unlocking padlocked fire doors
>   blazing a toxic swoosh of flame, a stitched-up
>   profit drive, no sprinkler dousing
>   incendiary sales-floor targets with
>   screams of branded immolation.

> *'[A] UN agency study found that nearly 60% of Burmese labourers toiling in its seafood processing industry were victims of forced labour.'*
> – The Guardian, 14 December 2015

How many souls is my seafood worth?
>   The sous-chef has no measure for that,
>   for freeing tuna slaves trawled gross,
>   for netting children like the shrimp they peel,
>   manacled in icy desperation
>   as the plankton of the food chain, invisible
>   footnotes on a corporate balance sheet.

The Landing

Carolina Massie
Belgium

Shortlisted for the 2018 International Literary Prize

Landing in Lewes, on earth.
Toes crunch dry grass underfoot,
Breezy bunting whispers its greeting, soft sunlight kissing our cheeks,
Filtering through rainbow wind chimes glistening, tinkling their welcome
To Tribal Earth families.

A sigh, a chai, so high
On warm love
For all
And no one in particular
Warm up of airwaves and airways. Sound check.
A beat begins. Baboom. The Music starts.
A voice
So pure. Rising, Haunting via ears,
Piercing sternum, revealing a read, pulsating heart,
Open with fat, salty, summer raindrop tears.
Drum beat picks up momentum -Badooma badooma badooma badap-
Swaying, on feet, on earth

Hips and hearts bewitched, bespasmed
The band, like a 50s gentleman, a Shamanic magician
Enchantingly inviting us to dance to
Urban Tribal rhythm vibrations

Kakatsitsi pounds power djembes,
Blood pumps through a healthy heart,
Alive, easy dread-lock spirit,
Cherries passed around,
Badooma badap
Smiling each exhale as blood turns to fire.
But
Lethal cherry pit, hard as bullet
Shatters marshmallow world in which we floated
Sharp metal tears constrict throats
Airwaves close. Anaphylactic shock asphyxiates.
An ambulance.
Beep. Beep…
"Wait outside please." Glared at by critical, fluorescent lighting and dirty linoleum floors.
Beep. Wait. Beep.

Beep. Beep. Steroids. Beep.
Shaken bottle of pop body
Hisses its relief
Upon kissing bottle-opener meds

Breath comes back.

The Shaman's Benz brings back the beat

Black, winding, narrow roads

Our journey back -life musing its contrasts-

to wind chimes, deep, endless stars and warm hugs

From concerned friends, the grass and the earth.

Ypres

Ian McDonald
United Kingdom

Shortlisted for the 2018 International Literary Prize

"Reduced to ruins no higher than a man…"
The caption on the photo not quite true;
A stump of tower, an archway and some stones,
But in the background nothing, nothing you could name.
A devastation so complete you'd think
Four thousand years had done this, not just four.

The names of those who died here are inscribed
Upon the famous gate. Remembered, honoured,
Ritualised at the setting of each sun.
Yet to my mind the heroes of this place
Are those who lived, returned, cleared up the precious
Rubble, washed their hands and built again.

They must have known the best they could achieve
Would be a sort of movie set in which to live,
A simulacrum of their home, not real,
A photograph in stone of what it was.

Endangered Words

Alison McNulty
United Kingdom

Shortlisted for the 2018 International Literary Prize

The more you look the more they hide
as you research internal word bank,
it is a tantalising paradigm.

They escape wriggling through shallows
as black tadpoles hiding in rock shades.
So you're forced to ignore them for a while.

Considering this I recall
Darwin's letters – Kew's treasured
possessions – how they had been written

using black gall ink that's now corroding,
forming haloes in his ascenders,
d, struggling for existence, becomes a.

His cross-written theories could waterfall
from their page, facing complete extinction.
As from throat pool frog pops out – a fully
formed case of natural selection.

Thunder Over Blair Atholl

Laurence Morris
United Kingdom

Shortlisted for the 2018 International Literary Prize

I have dreams which are born of hills,
Sustaining echoes of the enduring power
Of that first mist-kissed glimpse
Of an elusive summit, or of spying,
Down from an ice-crowned pinnacle
To the twisted path of an upland river,
A brief prospect of some distant world.

Fleeting visions it is true, and far from lucid,
But still enough to power me
Down the turnpike roads, and bring life
To the sapping office hours,
Memories as precious as the primroses
I once surprised, radiant with life,
Snug in the clasp of a Knoydart glen,
Or the thunder I heard, late one summer,
Tolling loud above Blair Atholl.

And, if as I was told today,
There is no remaining solitude
But mere degrees of poverty,
And if God will not finish creation
Until the last man is truly dead,
And if isolation is by now impossible,
Then it is still some consolation
To chart the course of streams,
And dream on hills,
To know both grace and rapture.

2 Poems

Pukhraj Neogi
India

Editor's Choice of International Entries

1.

IN THE THROES OF RAINBOW PASSION

In the azure skies of ardour,
Soars high,
White dove of my soul,
Fluttering innocently,
Into arms of its true love,
With amber oneness of heart and mind,
Like snowflakes in spring time.

It's neither pink inside out,
Nor blue all through and through,
But it feels blue in a pink Body,
In a world colour blind,
To all the colours in-between.

Alas, Burying the rainbow passions,
Deep in the heart of scarlet earth,
Bereft of any tenderness,
Where the stake of homophobia pierces, through my white Dove,
Leading my soul far away
Into the grey haze of dictates.

2.

BLACK ROSE

Grey mist
Shrouds the hills
Running parallel
Across the river
Whose gushing dark waters
Teasingly Flow
Between the gloomy banks
The only witness
Is an abandoned cottage
Home to a wheatear
Covered green in algae
Drooping lower every season
Ravaged by time
Breathing ruggedly
Yet Held together
By an untamed garden
Of wild berries and shrubs
Silently
Grows a black rose
Every spring.

Father

Val Ormrod
United Kingdom

Shortlisted for the 2018 International Literary Prize

I watch you sitting under the willow tree,
sunlight shimmering through restless leaves
to freckle your still handsome face.
A soft summer breeze winnows
the lustrous hair that belies
your advancing years.
Your eyes, once so bewildered,
are no longer fearful; you are cocooned
in the rhythm of the garden.
A smile settles, serene upon your face
as your fingers stray to caress
our old retriever resting at your feet.
There is a calming inside my chest
like the thickening of honey, the humming
of bees, the slow turning of ivy to crimson.
It's been ten years now, but still I see you
sitting there beneath the willow tree,
haloed by the setting sun.

Did Socrates Dream of Kenny Dalgish?

Ian Rollitt
United Kingdom

Shortlisted for the 2018 International Literary Prize

The world, some say, is a dream

the dream just a construct of our minds

beyond this are our bodies, and even even our souls

dancing, dancing, true beauty

the mystery our dream has yet to unravel.

In this world we have dreamed

I used to dream also of big things

like the sky and fame.

How little I knew.

On the ridge to Lose Hill

the sun is a river of light on the windows of Hope.

My limbs are supple

and I am pleased with my sweat.

At this very moment my wife is somewhere

else out there in the Peaks

walking a marathon for charity

last night I coached my boy's football team.

When did we start doing this?
When did we dive into the turquoise sea?
Perhaps it is not necessary to be
perhaps all we need is the dream.
Let the birds have the sky!
I've seen Socrates play
the Brazilian one, I mean
I understood his brilliance
and boldly I claim
a little of it passed into me.
Once in a blue moon
I'm even Kenny Dalglish on the half-turn
and now that's what I coach – the half-turn
and one day they might see footage of King Kenny
and they'll understand.

And by the grace of the dream
we will still be here
dreaming of the quantum
so dissolved by love
that our minds and bodies are never apart
dancing, dancing, never apart.

Afternoon Tea

Christine Rowley
United Kingdom

Shortlisted for the 2018 International Literary Prize

What time do we leave

I say with glee

I'm looking forward to afternoon tea.

Just after noon

That's very soon

It's a very long way, you see.

We get to nan's

I'm her number one fan

As she puts on such a spread.

She opens the door

It's now around four

I'm hungry and crave to be fed.

At the age of five

I'm very alive

Full of confidence and cheek.

I try to sit still

But wriggle I will

Can we eat now please I speak.

In a minute or so

To the table I'll go

Ready for jam and bread.

I try a book

Then I take a look

At what's on the table instead.

I hope I'll see

A treat just for me,

So I have a good look around

It's not there on a plate

It must be a mistake

I'll search this needs to be found.

44 | PRECIOUS

I open a door

And sit on the floor

Looking at my favourite spread.

Salmon, I need

Please Nanny I plead

To go on my favourite bread.

My mum's in sight

I see Angel Delight

Chocolate whipped up just for me.

My eyes open wide

I've got nothing to hide,

Can we add it to afternoon tea.

Happy as a cat,

I run around the flat

Picking up sweets that I see

Then it's Thank you! Bye, bye!

Til next time I cry

Oh how I love afternoon tea.

Lullaby of Old Northumberland

Raymond Salisbury
United Kingdom

Shortlisted for the 2018 International Literary Prize

Our Gerald is nine,
   the bairn'a me brother,
which makes'us 'is Aunty
   when ah feel like 'is Mother

Fa torn kecks an' barked knees
   ya'll n'ah find 'is equal.
An' it's darnin' 'an plasters,
   after tea, as a sequel.

'Ha'ya jam pot ta lend us?'
   he says, grinning at me.
'Why, aye, Bony Lad,
   but where at'll ya be?'

'Wi' a lass ta the burn. . .
   from up the big 'ouses .'
'Well watch thy sel', then

an' mind them school trousies.'

Then 'e's off like a whippet
   down't road pen'n'inkin'.
' 'e's up to no good,'
   I'm stood there an' thinkin'.

Long shadows of ev'nin'
   When, on the back step,
' a jar full'a berries,
'e's left'us, the Pet.'

'Wll ya look what 'e's left us?'
   the man's in the tub
an' 'e growls back an answer,
   an' then off to the Pub.

'A whole lotta nice ones,'
   an' ah'm raking the fire,
when in comes 'is Mam,
   breathin' lungs full of ire.

'Will ya credit young Gerald,
   an' what 'e's bin doin'?
We'll nay 'old'us 'eads up,
   fa big troubles a'brewin'.

' 'twas Schoolteacher's yang'un,
   by't burn in the bushes
wi blood on 'is pants.
   I say, "What ya think this is?"

Is 'e worried? Not 'im.
   Not the slightest concern.
I ask ya. . . in't dark,
   wi a lass by the burn?'

So I says to 'er straight,
   she's glarin' at me,
'the clues in the bushes,
   'e went for a pee.'

An' I show 'er the berries,
   luscious, red as can be'
an' she turns away, sheepish,
   an' can't look at me.

And I bid 'er 'Goodnight'
   and remind 'er 'e's nine,
'an boil up the berries,
   an' wish 'e were mine.

The Elemental Selfhood

Margarita Serafimova
Bulgaria

Shortlisted for the 2018 International Literary Prize

Let us smell of our passions!
Smell of plays with octopuses
and of sex with beloved men!
And of a muddy sea that reaches from one end
of all things to the other;
that we who like it like our blood
cannot drown in.

Just Another Kid

Samuel Shapiro
United States

Shortlisted for the 2018 International Literary Prize

Just another kid,
Anxious to know how I did,
Already know the answer cause I didn't study shit.
Throw a fit? That'd make me a hypocrite.
Possess some feelings I need to omit.
She put a smile on my face. Bought me a banana split.
When I walk into class, I feel like I don't fit in,
How's everyone readin' so fast, damn im dim,
Society got me feelin like school's vital above all,
Skipped happiness along the way, guess i'll play my lil' violin.
Spent a lot of time outside, alone, happy with a ball,
Pain is temporary, a true feeling from within.
Natural to wanna hide, amid the craziness inside,
Who am I? A question, that's implied.
It's up to me to decide what I want magnified.
Progress over Pride. Progress over Pride

Sea Trove

Lizzie Smith
United Kingdom

Shortlisted for the 2018 International Literary Prize

The twinkle of speckles of sand,
Cascading in the sunlit wave,
A pearl inside a nacred shell,
The diamonds of salt between rocks,
Silver moonlight playing,
The antique piles of rocks
Secreting ancient ammonites,
Cowrie shells used as coin,
The abounding blue gold of water,
The harnessing of the Zephyr breeze
And the towering tidal wave -
From the ebony boom of thunder
To the most intricate seahorse:
These are the treasures of my kingdom.

The Colour Blue

Ted Stanley
United Kingdom

April finds me in the woods again
Dark earth sifting through my fingers
Rich memories drifting through my mind

All that is lost
All that remains

The dark earth hue
The flowers few
The shades of you
The colour Blue

Pharaoh

Tim Taylor
United Kingdom

Shortlisted for the 2018 International Literary Prize

Proud I was in life, but foolish, believing crowns
and flattery were signs of real power.
But scarcely was my chamber dug
when I was sent to dwell in it.
Here, I was meant to dine in splendour with the gods
but gold and jewels have no sheen
in endless dark: what use are chariots
and hunting bows inside this womb of stone
that drip-feeds me its cursed gift of ever-life?
Disembowelled, bound, and blind
how I have known the infinity of night!
You come as thieves:
I do not care – these things are yours.
Gladly, I exchange them for your gifts, of space, of light.

Tiny Choirboy

Laura Theis
United Kingdom

Winner of the 2018 International Poetry Prize

we came in from the dark & on our night-time walk we had seen
so many spooky black trees that ghosts seemed a real possibility

(that's when I first saw you)

surrounded by figures in white robes - eidolons maybe, slowly advancing,
beckoning us into the candle light, you led the way and we followed
in silence: our trust rewarded in the gold of a cold college chapel filled
with evensong from a dozen throats & I saw your earnest face aglow
with concentration - saw it disappear as you sat down -
that's how tiny you were

(and my life was yours)

you see something about your innocent joy as you joined in with
the angelical song in such a secret, mysterious place had reminded me
with bewildering force of someone, someone...

(my unborn son)

Jewels

Julia Wallis
United Kingdom

Shortlisted for the 2018 International Literary Prize

We husband health and intimacy now.
Like misers, ekeing out a cherished cache.
Savouring the short-lived glow of each vivid rich ruby:
Plucked from its purse, exposed to shared delight,
Tumbled in the cups of our palms.
Then stashed against the dearth to come.

No words will tell our story when you go,
And my last memories leave, like jewels
Pounded to dust, and stolen by wind-shear.
Trapped-in-amber moments on sun warmed cliffs,
Rock, parching saltwater from sea-drenched skin.
Bodies not tanned, toned, nor superhuman.

Although together, we were immortals:
Ready to respond, always, to a look,
A skimming touch, the scent of stunted pines.
Smouldering forest fire crackling to life.

No notion then, of quotas for life–joys.
Of our ration of breaths dwindling.

Memories wither with stiffening muscles,
Rats gnaw our hoard beneath the boards.
Together, we plotted exploits. No warning,
As we served indentured hours, that our
Allotted potency would be clawed back —
By wrinkled talons: mirrors of our selves-to-be

No beryl from the midnight sun, or
Jade of Northern lights. No memory gems
Of turtles rowing in sibilant surf.
Or onyx whales' eyes off the Isle of Mull.
No more pearls of sharing hours together,
To salt away for grey days and cruel nights.

Still, a deep glow, in each erratic breath,
Prehistoric hunters' treasured kindling.
Nurtured and nursed by each of us.
Now, we husband health and intimacy,
Like misers, questing for an opal meet:
Tranquil, by a brook in dwindling spate.
While trying not to miss recollections,
Already blown to dust.

Dancing in the Rain

Rachel Wilkins
United States

Shortlisted for the 2018 International Literary Prize

The sky cast down rain.
"Trees ain't a good umbrella,"
She laughed to herself,
for whilst the world bunkered down,
she danced in the balmy tears.

Precious Long Ago

Sadie Wood
United Kingdom

2nd in the 2018 International Poetry Prize

I live in a place
Where unwanted children go
How I got there is a question
An answer I don't know

I suppose my mum loved me first
But then thought otherwise
I don't ask questions
Because I know I'll be told lies

I don't remember much from before
Not their faces, not much anything
All I can recall to mind
Is a song they used to sing

'Come sweet child, golden hair
Lime green eyes blushing deep
We love you dearly
Never weep

58 | PRECIOUS

We love your laugh

You beam and you glow'

And that song is why I think

I was precious long ago.

Hourglass

Safiyyah Yacoobali
United Kingdom

Shortlisted for the 2018 International Literary Prize

Trickles of warmth
bronze her musky skin

Sandy shades of copper
surrender in the desert sun

Ephemeral reflections emerge
from a forever changing sea

Dunes trace
past pilgrimages

Seeking tomorrow's
severed shadows

I envelope sand
in my soft embrace

PRECIOUS

The ripples whisper

"Beware o' bedouin,
the sands of time begin"

speckles like ballerinas
dance through my diastemas
fleeting
like gold dust
like life

From 'Red Hawthorn-Hedged'

Paul Sutherland
United Kingdom

IV

When did I first long for the here and now?
I stared for miles from the rear side window
of my father's car; saw the moon
for the first time as free
a winged-horse in silver disguise,
motoring as fast as dad's Pontiac
far advanced in age. Comfortable
in that tasselled-textured backseat
I had no yearning to return home.
I filled up with all that I watched
the rear glass' soft curve sharing
curved muscles of that night-galloper.
I begged the journey not to end.
Here I am, after decades of journeys
gazing from a train's round-cornered glass
still hoping for non-arrival, the sacred
in-between-ness of here and now.

HAMMOND HOUSE

A social enterprise membership organisation founded by students at the University Centre Grimsby and run by volunteers. We aim to encourage and support creative talent in art and literature providing opportunities for members to showcase their work and develop a successful career.

Our current activities include Publishing, Literary Competitions, Film Making, TV Production, Writing Workshop, Festivals and Community Engagement Programmes.

Members benefit from reduced competitions fees, and opportunities to showcase their work or get involved in our range of creative activities.

We are planning to offer a range of publishing options to new writers, and expand our programme of engaging with isolated people in both rural and urban the communities through art and literature

www.hammondhousepublishing.com

2018 International Literary Prize

The third year of this prestigious literary prize saw a record number of entries spread across five continents.

WINNER	**Something Else**	**Sophie Kirkwood**
2nd Place	Ewigkeit	Sean O Suilleabhain
3rd Place	Motor Skills	Gordon Aindow

JUDGES
Peter True, Anjali Wierny, Hugh Riches, Alex Thompson, Sarah Hunter-Carson, Adrian Mills and Steve Jackson.

Awarded by the University Centre Grimsby

Sponsored by Kenwick Park Estate: Golf Hotel and Spa

HAMMOND
HOUSE

www.hammondhousepublishing.com

University Centre Grimsby

2019 International Literary Prize

1st Prize £100
2nd £50
3rd £25

Worldwide Publication
for the top 25 poems

Theme: LEAVING
Poem of 2000 - 5000 Words
Entries open 6th February 2019
Submission deadline 30th September 2019

OTHER 2019 COMPETITIONS

International Short Story Prize
International Screenwriting Prize

HAMMOND HOUSE

www.hammondhousepublishing.com

University Centre Grimsby

The University Centre Grimsby, as part of the Grimsby Institute, is built on high expectations, a focus on learning, commitment to achievement and an engaged, practical education for all students.

A wide range of degree level courses are available including BA (hons) Creative and Professional Writing.

www.grimsby.ac.uk

KENWICK PARK ESTATE
Golf Hotel and Spa

Country house hotel in 320 acres of woodlands, parks, and manicured grounds with woodland lodges, club spa, evergreen spa, tennis courts and championship golf course. The perfect place to relax and recuperate

www.kenwick-park.co.uk

BILLBOARD TV

Theatre, Music, Movies, Art and Literature

BILLBOARD is produced by members of the Hammond House group at the University Centre Grimsby, including students from the creative arts, media and writing faculties, graduates, and members of the local community.

The programme covers Theatre, Music, Arts and Literature across the Humber region, going behind the scenes of your favourite shows, reviewing the latest film releases, books and art exhibitions, interviewing local celebrities and showcasing local musicians.

Billboard provides a great opportunity to showcase member's skills and pursue the Hammond House mission to encourage local talent and engage with the local people.

Broadcast frequently on range of popular TV channels and always available at www.billboardtv.uk

www.billboardtv.uk

HAMMOND HOUSE

OTHER PUBLICATIONS

ETERNAL – Award-Winning Poetry from around the world from our 2017 International Poetry Prize
CONFLICT - Award winning short stories from our 2016 International Literary Prize
WHO'S AFRAID OF THE DARK - Illustrated children's story featuring augmented reality
SHAKESPEARE IN DEBT - Hilarious Elizabethan farce

FORTHCOMING PUBLICATIONS

COWS IN TREES – Witty account of a vet at large
MEMORIES OF RURAL LINCOLNSHIRE FAMILIES AND THE GENTLEMAN EXECUTIONER – Family history

FORTHCOMING FILMS

Hammond House Productions

SPIN – An undercover policewoman is torn between life and duty. Featuring a replica of one of the most expensive cars in the world, the Ferrari 250 SWB California

EIGHT BALL – Winner of the 2018 University Centre Grimsby International Screenplay Prize. Candidate for the Asthetica Film Festival.

www.hammondhousepublishing.com

www.ingramcontent.com/pod-product-compliance
Lightning Source LLC
Chambersburg PA
CBHW030457010526
44118CB00011B/977